SAMSARA AT QUANTUM ZENO

SAMSARA

AT

QUANTUM

ZENO

Gabriel Gómez

Contents

So the darkness shall be the light,
and the stillness the dancing.

–T. S. Eliot

For Hilary

ÉMIGRÉ

On the elegant field

A string of mustangs

Explode as they appear

Discolor the atmosphere

In Kinhin, left hand

Orbits solar plexus

Shining gem empties to sepia

We wander alien plains

Firm abdomen, straight neck

We circuit the earth

Our Spanish doesn't match

Your opulent rolling pronunciations

One leg surrenders while another awaits

And I do not

I do not blossom

Euclid's Common Notion
Haiku Element Variations: Collaboration with Donald J. Trump

A. Things which equal the same thing also equal one another

These aren't people
They're bringing drugs, bringing crime
These are animals

Mexicans are a sequence of galaxies

Collapsing in the absence of light

Mechanically sound, bent at the knees . . . leagues of us

Our Jesus, enshrined in portraits, shimmers with Pledge

We dance on skeletal truss in the world

Harvesting rainwater is illegal in most western states

Migratory birds follow one innate idea after another

These plains were oceans where we move throughout

Serif cleft, vowels, verbs, names in Spanish to follow

B. Things that coincide with one another are equal to one another

Prosecute parents
Coming in illegally
Take children away

(People of the) accordion bellow, Norteña through honeycombed fence

(People of the) outline of fencing visible from space

(People of the) tectonic events, major rock suites, peeling limestone

(People of the) public bathrooms, Fabuloso cleaner, notes of pine, plastic seats

We're one seizure, a movement still

                                        You are so conquest, parallel lines in the west

                                    You are so academic, self-enamored, tenure track

(You are the) slender boat, war films, wave crests

(You are the) color of fading, open windows

(You are the) invasive species, choke in the wheat

You are renamed when discovered

You are snow, glisten, dissipate in the air

You bivouac, make notes, bounce

C. If equals are subtracted from equals, then the differences are equal

Legal immigrants
Want border security
We must build a wall

One metric foot aflame among the old water

We're old weight in an old imprint

The maker of steps onto the alien moon

Oh, I thought you were Honduran . . . .

Always crossing this former ocean

And always cockle remains and petroglyph

Caked alters unfamiliar with dust

Into bread then the great mud wall

D. If equals are added to equals then the wholes are equal

Want a great country
We want a country with heart
Know they can't get in

Codex of Permanence: A Sunday Shopping List

- Huevos
- Jalapenos curtidos
- Tomate
- Cebolla
- Ajo
- Chile de arbol
- Knorr Suiza
- Café
- Arroz blanco
- Sopa de fideo
- Marias
- Salsa de tomate
- Frijoles
- Laurel
- Masa de maiz
- Carne de res
- Chorizo
- Pan dulze
- Azucar
- Pollo
- Una es-pri or wink

E. The whole is greater than the part

The system is full
We can't take you anymore
Sorry, turn around

Begin erasing

Shelve strategies to move

Shoes, textured belts, Huipil

Battle monstrous intuition

Stay. Scale the footprint

Gas bill. Paper checks

Your earth is magnetic

You ground the circuit.

License to drive.
>>>>>>>>>>>>Sunday drives
>>>>>>>>>>>>wine tasting
>>>>>>>>>>>>river rafting
>>>>>>>>>>>>holiday foods

Pendulum swings in God's favor
When favor and God are done

Some, I assume, are good people

A HUNGER FOR SOMETHING LIKE PRAYER

A boy is words in chorus.
Lunges the lips, listens.

A conversation. Surgically precise.
Phrasing pauses. Breathes than/then speaks.

Less of himself copied. Sits zazen in transcript.
Less so in translation. Then all collapses.

She's leaving. Another country. It's far.
Time has stopped. Its math has stopped.

Without architecture building starts. Edges
untangle. She is distance, sentence, stanza.

Sand is everywhere . . . .

A new metric foot is awake
Whales breach. Birth then Rebirth.

Sit. Carve to posture. Swell into volume.
Let her take it. Let her take it all.

Into a pair of hands, Mondrian segments
They pulse with blood of a spring pile under winter asparagus

Strange, as the garden greens and circular hum of
Hidden bulbs that lie concentric and divided in sleep

More so, how pearly callouses disturb the palm
Grip the voice box as it prepares to sing

Innate lines of migratory duck and railroad truss
Twist out of frames, farmer orange, quail-egg blue

That old wave hits once and dissipates again
To have known between our now your then

Of cresting frequencies, of octave loop
Vibrating reed, thyroid and chamber, preparing for noise

Wait for the sound to anneal, adjust to us

You dress how I thought you would dress

Smoke and fragrant lilac flooding the open air

It's summer, I think. Expository, I think.

Somewhere in a field its smoke will animate

Unspooling the hunger of us

Our frequency under the branches

Yes, they are booms collecting our sound

We once knew everything about the world
Through dramatic irony and the divine

A covenant softened with dim light made us
Believe mothers, like you, were enveloped in grace

Beginning one activity in English then ending
In vowels dropped and silent ch, e, and p

A trembling cask spurred by the spirit, wrapped her roomy bloodstream
Her bounce, it hardens, over the sidewalk, until she is

In my room, when I saw the shirt coming over your arms
And shoulders, I barely noticed you were drowning;

I merely thought you were saying "yay!"

After an afternoon of light decay
Comes a voice with treble
Control burn is eye shadow blue
Raku birds shatter back to dust
I accent out the shadowy words
The landscapes pans, exit music.

Become the arms
Become the grasps
Apply limbs
There you are
Reassure me

Rhythmic models
Arrested bursts
Becoming stars

Stellar wiles
Roaming tongue
Wings and wire

Your movement is flesh
Drawn to redrawn

                              of cornered light
                              of tilting axis
                              of buoyant frame

We halo the earthy smoke inside our mouths
Until our tongues swell to the cheek with it

We pretend to listen to the high treble of the AM station, oldies,
Duke of Earl, Gene Chandler from the F-150 tailgate

A familiar turn of phrase while we muse language
A singer building somewhere else with words

Walking upon the elk carcass
Its bones disheveled like laundry
By the mountain lion
As it drank its haunches
Tightened before its
Underbelly was split open
Onto the river this afternoon
The eye's coagulant puckered face
Ate the clouds like soup

Rectangle of their bodies

An ascendant pile, photographs

A portrait from my grandfather, 18, Clint, TX

It's 1928, Sunday, when the idea of a portrait struck him

Broad shoulder blades eclipse the tender spine

The wrinkled knuckle at peace

The house breathed in plumes

Inhaled the sweet alfalfa

Scooped the last air out of its lungs

The tree line gone for good and last

Splintered wood into an ordered pile
Its web of these rough constellations

End bits are burned in a mesh
Singing the first songs of August

Model airplanes of your opening hands
Break into rhyme schemes and the sculpture of sex

It's shocking how anything of beauty would result
From those thunderous waves

Machines at peace once amped about the hills
A voice with heft maps the cooling charges
Veins coerced from the ground in Mexico a kinetic of
Heaps and slag between movements
Ash, vigorous, thrown over the lot of us waiting somewhere

How the bone embossed the skin
Its sloping note braiding arms and hands
Shattering into specks of salt
How your song, too far afield, collapsed
Turned fizzy when we lost signal through the trees

Samsara at Quantum Zeno

Let's watch what they watch
They land, break and blanch
Spit and twist the words

Christen thee on my behalf
I mirror the sea, there once
Was sea and here it was

Volver, Volver, Volver
A tus brazos otra vez
Llegaré hasta donde estés

Seconds between seconds stop
We're on Earth and time will
Stop for us. We'll not decay

The cycle of then, samsara
Will live and die and ignite
Round particles billow

Under our skin and boil
I will end like starlight
Mid-travel, mid-sentence

I am segments in a
Desert walking north I
Don't pretend to know

What or who came before
I or us. Only know the place has
Been trampled upon for

Centuries and know that
Poetry won't soften thirst
Let's not pretend its death

Let's pretend the math and
Symbol match, somehow
Predict, when movement

Stops, our movement dies
And roots and grows, and
Stays, for the love of God

Stays, the particles rest, breathe
Lunar cycles, waves and births
We see our names. Say stay still.

We are the Jornada de Muerto
Bodies and the score of bones
Radiant in cactus bulbs

Of monsoon and prayer
Slouching empire crown
Pilgrims, scared and caged

Paused awkward. Arrested.
Socorro means help

Father, now I am become Death
The destroyer of worlds. Our
Mouths open the flowering tide

What births are here for [us]?
What dharma is here for [us]?
Your womb, another sun

[Border]

[Latino]

[Latina]

[Stop]

SWEETWATER

Out of reach for the current language
Alphabet curve softened on the palate
Notes of a terroir: distant vapor, lemon cake
Over the west all days end in the vacillant bow
Scribbles some dusk in our likeness

Save the draw of deer
Galloping toward cars
What sound must stir
Foraging their snouts
Compels them onward

Our structure is warp and weft to their science
Begins pulling, buoys a remarkable spot
Where centuries of ash no longer loop from prairie fire
Where centuries of thought, between our teeth, are in play

Layover

I'm too tired to ask for directions
Ask for food or a toothbrush or pen
Squint the digital list of flights
Then origami sleep on benches

Saint of beautiful non-related things
Restless planes plunging from the sky into
Pirouette: waiting, yoga pants, duty free

When am I?
American. Biased.

I am

Broken English
Loose Leaf
Manufactured Air
Imperfect Light
Stainless River

Saints of a sort of math and incoherent songs
Keep the planes circling above us
Smarter people decoded this years ago

Wrung the wonder from it
Distilled the magic
Normalized its mechanics

Suffer through flight paths
Shorter distance. Shorter layovers
No threshold, rite of passage, baptism
I'm here. Just here.

According to the bulletin board
The Amazon is known as the lungs of the Earth
Where tenured tucum palms are meaningless
Except for their spiny bark and industrious fiber
The place, and I'm quoting, is full of life

Forget this as it begins
Disappointing sleep on planes
Things you've photographed and eaten
We transmute to data

Dream of echoing folding chairs
Of the parquet floors of Versailles

The science is soft but alarmingly accurate
The soul will stir the lungs
Slip quietly into our ears and confuse

Dream of yourself as puzzle as quark
Your face shapes in the curtains for others
Now there are two and we are its sun-bleach stains
Safety webbing in the glass beyond

A crane afloat and breathing
In its fiery wind sleeps or not
Markings on our bodies

They would have you believe that as
You conclude your life it's always best
To be comfortable, asleep, ambivalent.

A Chinese visa will cost $200 and remain valid for 10 years
You pass and there you lay in the Shanghai airport for hours
This repeats every few months

You begin to think of money in different ways. Dinner and drinks
Become in-country plane rides, bus tickets, change for tuk-tuks
And so you hide. Become invisible. Forget the taste of foods. Din of crowds.
"I thought you moved away," they repeat.

She had a daughter, had been married, searched for horizon like us all.
And you should probably know that we had an affair
And by design destroyed everything around us
Her buttons were marked: unbreak, unsuffer, unhide.

My father dies on the day that the food trucks typically line the parking lot.

The primary nurse attending to my father is employee of the month.

Peaking into the other rooms as you walk towards the lobby is a huge mistake.

Terrible paintings are comforting to the pregnant women walking the corridors.

I think of the freelance graphic designer who produces the cancer pamphlets.

The coffee is shit, abundant, and free.

Flight paths, in vivo, overseas, marking our progress. The voices of pilots on in-flight channels speak remarkable things. More comfort. More complexity. No reference or root words. I read about an illness among the blind where they can't sleep. There is no night, horizon, light cues. Only further night. Oceans beneath them passing.

The nurses checking my father's levels are on
Message to smile, provide comfort, stay chatty
The upcoming election is our prompt as we wait

I didn't pack and can only afford thrift store shirts, pants, belt
My sister's message was disheveled but surgical
Details evaporated to breathy pauses.
Turn off the music in the car to avoid giving this a soundtrack

When I was younger, a thirst for travel meant that I would want
To lick the sidewalks of foreign cities. Wanted them inside me. Wanted to
Consume them like the flesh of enemies; a virgin heart before a stone God.

As a boy, I tried to think of the most Caucasian name to write into my assignments at school. Thus, Don Anderson, my protagonist, became a composite of my sister's best friend's father and a clerk at 7-11; he was an accountant, a good Samaritan, a friend to the paper bag brown boys and girls of Lyndon Baines Johnson Elementary School.

Dear Reader: Apparently, you need to be fully dressed to be cremated, so as I retrieved the requisite underwear from my father's dresser and returned to the funeral home; I rehearsed saying to our account manager if it was against policy to go commando into glory. No one laughed when I said it for real.

I once learned, incorrectly, that death is a P&L statement

At an open mic night.

Weight distribution on airplanes is what keeps them in the air.

There's terror in the water between lands.

Line breaks and stanzas in poetry are the plating of a dish.

The cities of America
Are burning beneath us
Everyone ignores the signs
Park on the mediums
Squat underneath the caution tape
Jump meaningless fencing
Solitude evaporates
Run-off resumes
Glimpses of snow in April are all but gone

Between Days in the Spring Ephemera

Day 1

We're lost.

Walking further
just the same
ocean things
years in millions
evaporated, just gone
matted bivalves
ancient beds
dreams of us
where billionaires launch
into ether, eventually,
animal tracks appear
from the drought
trains circumvent
the dunes, knew then
not to disrupt
shimmering silica
open airspace
it's nothing for miles

Day 2

Dust is everywhere.

It does this funny
thing when
we walk past,
sticks to the brush
until rain, I guess, draws
it back to the ground
this one time, they tested
a bomb so powerful it
turned the sand to glass
stayed like that until
we found it, reflected us
made us look funny
stretched our faces
like pears and buttons
the laughs and bodies
became vapor, in fact,
an entire life here
repeats a mantra
erases continually
the bomb, oh yes,
they used it

Day 3

I think we've died.

I can't tell for sure
of course, now,
we're stripped
we look for signs that
reflect our faith, repeat
back to us the prayers
we cast, seems silly
this theatre, lights and
seats, happening to us
now, but I'm retelling
you, changing the order,
employing the diction
of our time, making
judgments of our past
blame us just the same

Day 4

No, I don't remember.

But want to believe that I
Was funny and charming
Provided a variety of entry
Points for others to engage
I've learned that emotionally
Intelligent people tend to be more
Successful in their lives
Balance, I've read, is key
Assuming you have more
Than one focus. Let's pray
Here, in front of the cameras,
They'll remember us, remember
You too

Day 5

Time is a funny thing.

Hear the blossoms turning
into old seeds, spore of
old truths, open and empty
I am your sentence
how many times did
we break up, daily, you say

Day 6

Mise en Place.

The Red Wattle pig draws
into circles like dogs, their ruby
hues vary from chemical sunset
to craft ale, according to the
breeding guide, the sows are
excellent mothers, abundant suckling,
babies left plump and oily
and so, the breed is meant
for eating and mating
a kind of artisanal beast,
and I suppose, to curve
the palate into thinking
its flavor profile in its slaughter
there's an exchange of loss,
its knowing for knowing our place,
our draw of light and moon, settling
under the earth where we grow
stop pretending how wrong we are
to die in place

Day 7

I learn that the muddy churn
makes it impossible to read
through drafts of the Mekong River;
the only proof of its depth
are the sandbars that appear
as the water level drops
lanterns and bonfires dot
the low specs, which are really
the high points in the river's path,
during the boat races
on the Nam Khan the bamboo foot
bridge is rebuilt every year
after the swollen river destroys it
during monsoons like clockwork
the French expats are effusive
with their descriptions in this
their hands punctuate their syntax
my rented motorbike cutting humidity
breath perfumed with anise
relaxed among the school of fish, absorbed into
the sound of motorbikes clutching in unison

Day 8

Mom would add bologna, jalapenos, water
in the blender, cut the crust from white bread
smear the mixture onto the canvas
and roll it up into little blankets, terrible sushi rolls
for my relatives, usually the old ones who arrived
at the evening parties when it was still daylight
the floors evaporating their fresh mop
my uncle would arrive with his accordion
he carried the instrument in its proper black
case that made it seem enormous and diplomatic
it would sit in a corner the entire evening until
the drinks had their predictable effect; he wouldn't
play music, only bits and chords, bent and affected, he
held it in his arms like the dying Christ in marble

Day 9

These squares of earth have been stomped upon
For centuries and no matter the manhandling
That accompanied its remains, a balance of elements
Laugh continually; temperatures drafted from the sea
Lime, water, aperture of sloping hills, are what they please
And yet the rows of fruit lay paragraphed in uniform syntax
Lettering specks in precise height against the gnarled root
Thrusting Chamberlain bouquets skyward
Dominion, or sex maybe, caused the urge for structure
Bugled in our blood at rut to pierce our knives
Of fruiting spurs to open the flower in control
Only slightly and coerce an image of wine from the
Terroir, protect her from danger, close her off
From our eyes and mouths as we drink

Day 10

I wasn't expecting to muse
About adding the word Mexican
Before sweet bread upending unspoken
Truths about place; how we are a complete
Terroir, roots forward, in everyplace

I chewed and sipped and agreed to wait
For the weather to change to my liking
To think about unexpected things, to
Add me into the universe where I
Lived long without papers, to step out
In the cold and accept it for what it is

Day 11

Minutes after the draw of sunrise
We came to a stop. Leapt from the car.
New Mexico by the edges of Great Plains
And a multitude of miles, where we can all agree,
Nothing much happens, and yet, the expanse
Can't help us escape from going inward,
Fixating on the space as a fenced rectangle
That it belongs to someone or something
That before any of us, the grasses, cared for nothing
Remain unchanged; they find it hilarious, I bet,
At our attempts to shape them into cosmology,
Bread, body, blood . . . eaten, repeated. Laugh until
It burns, faith I mean, boxing it up, and going nowhere

Day 12

Your previous lives went by
Different names. Back then,
You fancied symbols more than words
Your parents knew somehow
The point of what you were
Trying to get at with little effort
The way costumes exaggerate on stage
They work to announce you rather
Than tease out the finer more boring points
I was watching you eat, unintentionally, watching
You sleep, hoping that it would mean more
To be with you, instead, you fed me
Peyote tea, we chased each other until we dropped
Grew again on the earth that may have already
Hated us from before the exhaustion took
What little daylight broke through the cracks

Day 13

unthink the Sunday brunch with co-workers
the phone call; the mechanical voice of my brother
explaining the fall, the stairs, furniture layout
he posits my mother falling, injuring her head
how she succumbs to gibberish, confusion, fog

next is the language of doctors
new categories and timeframes
more diagrams, added projections
language of surgery and outcome
I visualize PowerPoints with my mother's
totality spatchcocked in line charts

this is Denver. A ten-hour drive from El Paso.
a five-hour drive from Santa Fe. It's remarkable
how we managed to split the time and distance
evenly from one another. Remarkable how the body
fails so grandly. Wonderous, still

the Camino Real would have been visible from space
but we wouldn't have known that then. We wouldn't have
the words to know how we looked upon ourselves
rambling through the desert artery sharing bones
wandering your memory in confusion

Day 14

the smell of sulfur is first
see the steam pumping
public hot springs in a year
of the pandemic, pummeled
with soakers preoccupied with wellness
selfcare; we are all abandoned, you think,
that when our parents die, we are left broken,
handmade paper floating in boiling water

Day 15

they butchered pigs next to the textiles
severed fish heads and eels in plastic tubs
meat puzzles, slick floors, stalls dimmed like runways
our teacher pointed out turmeric mounds and prahok vats
hunger and delirium, pitches of Khmer overpowered the decay
wasn't it until we returned to the outdoor kitchen
among strangers, to prepare a meal
we realized our longing to ingest the sound
of traversed rivers and porous stones
impossibility of ancient temples at sunrise
suddenly it made sense, until it didn't
eating lotus seeds in Cambodia
coercing sweet buttons from their blooms
made us feel less, rounded the kernel in our mouths
disappeared for this country of water

Covenant

I'm told that somewhere in Los Angeles, there are cholos playing basketball with tabs of acid in their socks; it absorbs into their skin as the sweat glands open like millions of minuscule tongues accepting Eucharist . . . peaking, I imagine, amid the squeaking Adidas; laughter undulating into something like a bark of a seal.

I'm not sure if I believe that story, because I am nothing if not focused on getting back in the car and away from this asshole, who charges more than the going rate for a tab of windowpane, but I pay my seven bucks, half listen to whatever he has to say and leave.

Learn to expect three things when driving past a catholic church while on drugs in El Paso, 2:00 am, 1992.

1. No matter what, absolution is more important than the 9 o'clock/3 o'clock hand position on the steering wheel. And despite the fact that riding with a guy I barely know—the same guy who redlines his Acura on from 3rd and 4th gear every time—crosses himself as we pass a church in the Sunset district. I'm swept into a current of debris that lifts as we drive past.

2. Just an observation, but braking is not unlike genuflecting when entering a pew, avoiding eye contact with the altar; the knees will ache when kneeling, and that's how you know it's working.

3. Somehow, driving past the house of God, the house of your mother, the house of your memories is more important than this excerpt. You shiver. The drugs, too, are working.

And when you read "The Merchant's Tale," years from now, there will be a moment when you understand the covenant between God and Man, when it speaks to you around the seminar table; the very hand that reached into Adam's oblique, removed his rib from the leathery sinew is now crowning your head, twisting it towards her in bliss, aroused in the swallow, her lips still pursed from the mouthful, you meet, again . . . eyes closed, inside her, awake in time to hear her say, "now."

ACKNOWLEDGMENTS

I want to thank the *Santa Fe Literary Review*, where some of these poems first appeared, and Mouthfeel Press for their continued support of my work.

ABOUT
Gabriel Gómez is the author of three poetry collections. He lives in New Mexico with his family. www.gabegomez.com

Samsara at Quantum Zeno

Mouthfeel Press is an indie press publishing works in English and Spanish by new and established poets and writers. We publish poetry, fiction, and non-fiction.

Cover Design and Interior Design: Kimberly James, www.kimmiejwrites.com

CONTACT **I**NFORMATION
Mouthfeelbooks.com
Info.mouthfeelbooks@gmail.com

ISBN: 978-1-957840-27-7
Library of Congress Control Number:
2 0 2 4 9 3 1 3 4 8

Published in the United States, 2024

First Printing in English
$18

9 781957 840277